Steve Parish KIDS

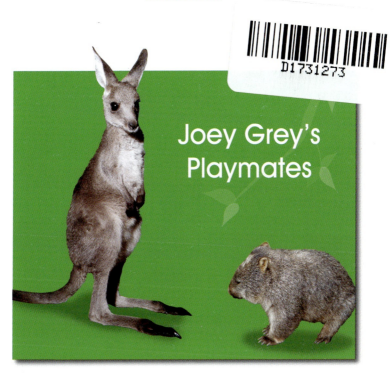

Joey Grey's Playmates

Joey Grey is too big to stay in Mum's pouch all day.

She climbs out
and gives herself
a scratch.

Scratch

Scratch

Scratch

She looks for her friend
Baby Wombat.

She can't see
Baby Wombat
anywhere, but she
can hear her…

Ah-choooo!
Ah-choooo!
Ah-choooo!

Can you see where
Baby Wombat is hiding?

She's hiding in the tree! "Hello Baby Wombat, do you want to play with me?" asks Joey Grey.

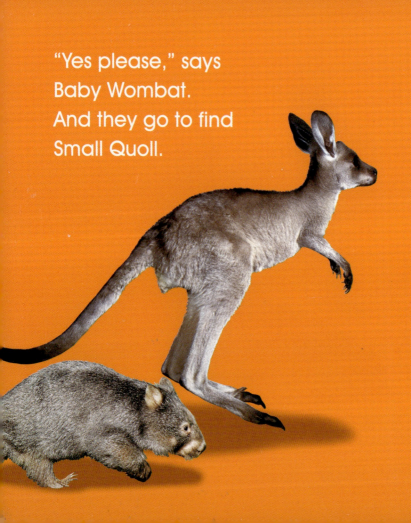

"Yes please," says
Baby Wombat.
And they go to find
Small Quoll.

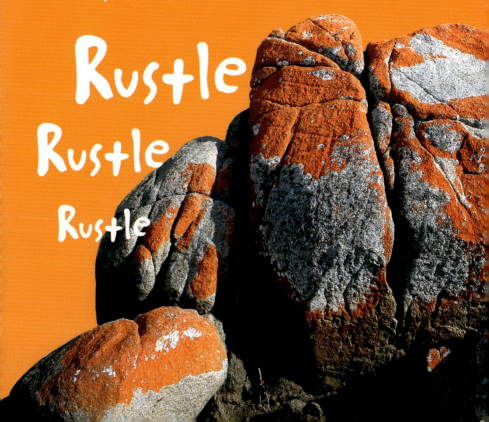

They can't see Small Quoll anywhere,
but they can hear her...

Rustle

Rustle

Rustle

Can you see where Small Quoll is hiding?

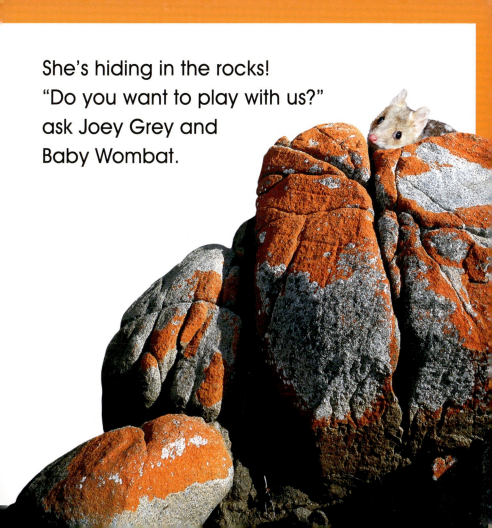

She's hiding in the rocks!
"Do you want to play with us?"
ask Joey Grey and
Baby Wombat.

"Yes please," says Small Quoll.
Joey Grey, Baby Wombat and
Small Quoll set off to find Koala.

They can't see Koala
anywhere, but they
can hear him...

Chomp!

Chomp!

Chomp!

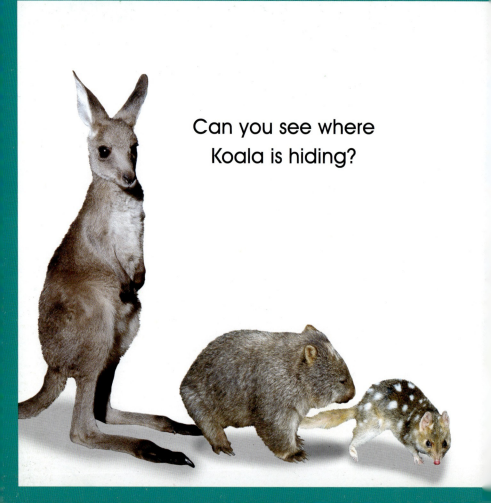

Can you see where
Koala is hiding?

He's in the tree!

"Do you want to play with us Koala?" ask Joey Grey, Baby Wombat and Small Quoll.

"Yes please," answers
Koala. Joey Grey and
Koala play catch.

Catch it!
Catch it!
Catch it!

Kick it!

Kick it!

Kick it!

Baby Wombat
and Small Quoll
play soccer.

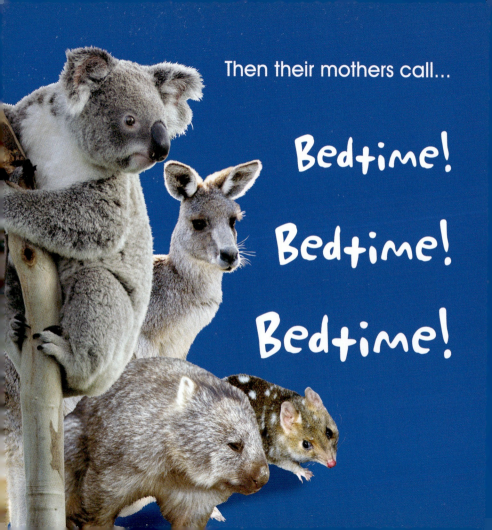

Then their mothers call...

Bedtime!

Bedtime!

Bedtime!

All that playing
has made the
babies sleepy.

Baby Wombat and Small Quoll go to join their mothers so they can go to bed.

Koala climbs onto Mum's back. Joey Grey hops into Mum's pouch.

ZZZZZZZZZZZ!

About Eastern Grey Kangaroos

Joey Grey is an Eastern Grey Kangaroo. These kangaroos live in mobs in the scrub, woodland and forest along Australia's east coast and in north-eastern Tasmania. During the day, they rest under shady trees. When it is cooler, in the early morning or afternoon, they come out to graze on grass. A mother Eastern Grey Kangaroo carries a joey in her pouch for around eleven months. Once the joey hops out of the pouch, it still drinks its mother's milk for another nine months.